Let's Investigate Sparkling, Silent Snow

Madelyn Wood Carlisle

Illustrations by Yvette Santiago Banek

FOREST HOUSE ®

School & Library Edition

All inquiries should be addressed to:
Barron's Educational Series, Inc.
250 Wireless Boulevard
Hauppauge, NY 11788

International Standard Book No. 0-8120-4736-2

Library of Congress Catalog Card No. 92-16832

Library of Congress Cataloging-in Publication Data

Carlisle, Madelyn Wood.
    Let's investigate sparkling, silent snow / by Madelyn Wood Carlisle;
illustrations by Yvette Santiago Banek.
        p.   cm.
    Summary: Discusses such aspects of snow as the shape of snowflakes, record
snowfalls, and how humans and animals adapt to snow. Also includes activities
and experiments.
    ISBN 0-8120-4736-2
    1. Snow—Juvenile literature.   2. Snow—Experiments—Juvenile literature.
[1. Snow.   2. Snow—Experiments.   3. Experiments.]   I. Banek, Yvette
Santiago, ill.   II. Title.
QC926.37.C37   1992
551.57'84—dc20   92-16832
                                                                    CIP
                                                                    AC

C. 1 1999
14.95

PRINTED IN MEXICO

2345 8800 987654321

Contents

Fun in the Snow 4

The Shapes of Snow 6

How Deep Is the Snow? 8

Where Does It Snow the Most? 10

Snow That Makes Rivers of Ice 12

Houses Made of Snow 16

How Animals Live with Snow 18

Snowshoes and Skis 22

Sleds and Sleighs 26

Sled Dogs 28

Can You Keep a Snowflake? 30

Fun in the Snow

Grown-ups complain about having to shovel it. It sometimes keeps cars, trucks, and even airplanes from moving. But for kids, snow is nothing but fun.

You can:

- Make snowmen with it.
- Throw snowballs.
- Build snow forts.
- Make snow angels.
- Slide down hills on sleds, snowboards, toboggans, inner tubes, shovels, or even pieces of cardboard.
- Glide over it on skis.
- Walk on it with snowshoes.
- Search for animal and bird tracks.
- Use it for science experiments.
- Or just look around at how beautiful the world is when it's covered with snow.

There are also a lot of things about snow that it's just fun to know!

Plenty of snow fell just in time for these children to try out their new toboggans.

Playing in the snow is fun for everybody.

The Shapes of Snow

Have you heard that no two snowflakes are shaped just the same? How can that be, when there are billions of billions of snowflakes falling all over the world? And how could we know that no two are alike when so few of them are ever looked at by anyone?

Well, a scientist has found two snowflakes that were just alike. She has pictures to prove it. The two snowflakes were joined together, side by side. So now if you hear someone say that no two snowflakes are *ever* the same, you can tell them that isn't true.

Snowflakes are crystals of ice. They start out as tiny specks that form when water in the air freezes. The specks float on the wind and bump into each other. They stick together. The clumps get bigger and heavier.

Usually the little specks of ice that stick together just grow into small, beautiful shapes. They are almost always hexagonal, which means that they have six sides or six points.

Would you like to know the names of some snowflake shapes?

The snowflakes that are like beautiful stars are called stellar crystals.

Some snowflakes start out as stellar crystals but change as they fall through a colder layer of air. Droplets of ice stick to them and give them odd shapes.

Plate crystals look like tiny six-sided plates.

Not all snowflakes are round or flat. Needle crystals are spear-shaped.

Sometimes several needle crystals stick together as they are falling.

The scientist who found two identical snowflakes took this picture of them.

Scientists study snowflakes by looking at them through microscopes.

There is another snow shape that is called a column crystal. It has six sides and flat ends. These crystals are often hollow, like a straw!

You can amaze your friends by naming the kinds of snowflakes that you catch on your mittens.

Photographs taken through microscopes reveal the beautiful shapes of snowflakes.

THE BIGGEST SNOWFLAKES

• In January, 1894, flakes more than 5 inches (13 centimeters) across startled people near Nashville, Tennessee.
• In March, 1900, strangely shaped rectangular snowflakes, nearly 3 inches (8 centimeters) in length, fell in Virginia.
• In January, 1912, snowflakes 3 1/2 inches (9 centimeters) across fell near Bristol, England.
• In January, 1915, 4-inch (10 centimeter) snowflakes fell in Germany.

Most falls of giant snowflakes occur in the coldest months of winter. But in England, in an unusual spring storm in 1951, the snowflakes that fell were 5 inches (13 centimeters) across.

How are these huge flakes formed? Scientists believe that they are created by electrical forces that join together hundreds, or even thousands, of ordinary snowflakes.

As far as we know, the biggest snowflakes ever seen descended from the sky more than 100 years ago in Montana. There, in January, 1887, giant saucer-shaped snowclumps were measured at 15 inches (38 centimeters) across and almost 8 inches (20 centimeters) thick!

If a snowflake like that ever fell on your head, you'd really feel it!

How Deep Is the Snow?

If you live in a place where it snows in the winter, it might be fun to keep a snowfall record.

Each time it snows, go out and measure the snow's depth. Just push a ruler or a yardstick down into the snow until it touches the ground. Be sure you pick a spot where the depth isn't less because the snow was blown away by the wind, or deeper because it was blown into a drift.

Each time you measure a snowfall, write down the number of inches in a notebook or on a calendar. At the end of the winter you can add up all the numbers and know how much snow fell where you live.

If *you* keep a snowfall record, you do it just for fun. There are snow surveyors who measure snow because that is part of their job. In those parts of the western United States where not much rain falls during the rest of the year, the people who live there always hope for heavy snow in the winter months.

If you go out to measure the snow depth, make sure the bottom of your ruler touches the ground.

Snow surveyors often use helicopters to take them into remote wilderness areas where they measure the depth of the snowpack.

Snow surveyors go up into the high mountains on skis, snowshoes, or in snowmobiles. They check the depth of the snowpack by reading the numbers on tall poles marked off in feet and inches. Everyone is happy when the snow is very deep because it means that in the spring, when the snow starts to melt, there will be plenty of water to fill the streams, rivers, and lakes. Some of the water is held back in big reservoirs and let out slowly into ditches. The ditches carry water to the fields all through the summer.

After a heavy snowfall, it may take hours to get cars out of garages and driveways.

Where Does It Snow the Most?

Many people who are asked "Where do you think it snows the most?" are sure they know the answer.

"The North and South Poles!" they say.

Actually, very little snow falls at either the North or the South Pole. The polar regions are really snow-covered deserts, where little moisture falls. They may get only a couple of inches of snow a year.

Why, then, is there so much snow covering the Poles?

Because it is so cold there that what snow does fall never melts!

This Alaskan island gets a lot of snow, but there are places farther south in the United States where more snow falls.

In a single snowstorm, 189 inches (480 centimeters) of snow once fell on California's Mt. Shasta.

The mountains of Washington, Oregon, and California get more snow than anywhere else. In a single snowstorm, 189 inches (480 centimeters) of snow fell at the Mt. Shasta Ski Basin in California.

The most snow that fell in one place in one twelve-month period was measured from early 1971 to early 1972. That was at Mt. Rainier, in Washington, where 1,224.5 inches (3,110 centimeters) of snow fell. That's over 100 feet (30 meters) of snow, enough to cover a nine-story building!

After a big blizzard, snowplows work around the clock to clear highways and city streets.

11

Snow That Makes Rivers of Ice

There are places other than the Polar regions where snow falls year after year and never melts completely. It gets deeper and deeper and heavier and heavier. Its weight squeezes it together and forces out the air trapped in the snow. The snow turns to solid ice. It has become a glacier. There are many glaciers in the high mountains of western North America.

At one time, long ago, glaciers covered almost all of what is now Canada and much of the northern United States. We call that time the Ice Age. Because the glaciers were formed from snow falling from the sky, it could just as well be called the Snow Age.

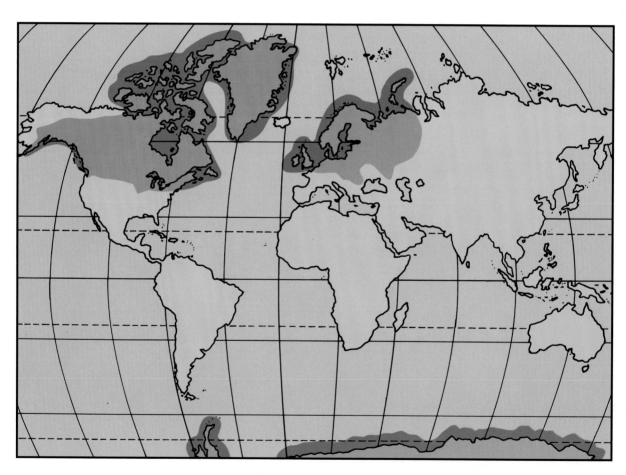

Was the place where you live once buried under ice? This map shows you how far the glaciers advanced during the great Ice Age.

This glacier in Alaska is moving slowly toward the sea.

13

A glacier is like a huge frozen river, sliding downhill. Glaciers move very slowly, maybe just a few inches a year. During the Ice Age, glaciers crept across the land, carving out hills and valleys as they went. In many places, lines on rocks show how they were scraped by a glacier and the stones it pushed across them.

Glaciers that are near oceans flow gradually to the sea. When big chunks break off and fall into the water, they are called icebergs.

An immense river of ice finally reaches Alaska's famous Glacier Bay.

A polar bear—at home on the ice.

Where is the world's largest glacier?

It's in Antarctica, where more than nine-tenths of the ice on Earth clusters around the South Pole. On that frozen continent, the Lambert-Fisher glacier system is the largest in the world. It is a river of ice that, in some places, is 40 miles (64 kilometers) wide. Altogether, this glacier system is more than 300 miles (480 kilometers) long.

When snow falls on a glacier, how long does it take for it to turn to ice?

When snow falls on the glaciers in the mountains of Europe and North America, it may take only five years for it to be packed down into the ice of the glacier. But in far northern or southern locations—such as Greenland or Antarctica—where temperatures are much colder, and where snowfalls are not so great, snow may fall and lie atop the underlying ice for as long as 3,000 years before the weight of the snow above it squeezes it down and turns it into ice.

How fast do glaciers move?

Most glaciers move very slowly, maybe only inches a year. But in 1982, Quarayaq Glacier in Greenland surged down its channel at the rate of 80 feet (24 meters) a day.

Houses Made of Snow

What do you think it would be like to live in an igloo, a house made of snow? To sleep inside it on an ice ledge covered with furs? Brrrrr! you are probably thinking. It would be much too cold! An American who lived with the Eskimos in Alaska for a while complained about the temperatures inside igloos. But he said they were much too hot! Hot and steamy, like it is in the jungle.

A long time ago, Eskimos and other people of the far North learned how to make houses out of snow. They had to, because there were no other materials out of which to build their homes. No trees grew where they lived. To make an igloo, they cut out chunks of hard-packed snow and used them as building blocks.

Eskimos away from home can quickly build an igloo for temporary shelter.

Eskimos no longer live in igloos, but they still know how to make them. Sometimes, when they are out on hunting trips, they build snow houses for shelter.

To keep warm inside an igloo they burn whale oil or fat. The fire is not big enough to melt the house, but it can cause a little of the snow on the walls to melt and evaporate. That is why it can be hot and steamy inside a house made of snow. When the fire is put out, the walls just freeze hard again.

Eskimos live with snow for most of the year. They have more words for snow than any other people. Here are some of them:

ah-ki-lu-kak Soft snow.

ah-put Snow in general.

i-gluk-sak Snow for a snow house.

i-ya-go-vak-juak Snowflakes.

kag-mak-sak Snow for piling up outside a house to insulate it.

ka-hik Falling snow.

ki-mik-vik Snow that has drifted unevenly.

ku-ah-li-vuk Snow that freezes as it falls.

mang-uk-tuk Snow that is getting soft.

ma-sak Wet snow.

msu-yak Deep, soft snow.

piek-tuk Drifting snow.

pu-ka Snow like salt, that doesn't stick.

sa-ki-ut-vuj Snow falling straight down.

ti-vi-gut Snowdrifts.

People can be cozy and warm inside a house made of snow.

How Animals Live with Snow

When winter comes and the snow gets deep, some animals migrate to places where less snow falls. When snow gets up to an animal's chest, it has trouble moving. Even some of the largest animals of the north country, like musk ox and elk, often go to places where the snow is not so deep.

Musk ox are huge animals, but their legs are short. Long-legged moose can more easily get around in deep snow.

These big animals have to be able to run to get away from the wolves that hunt them. They also have to paw through the snow to get at the moss and lichens they eat.

Can you imagine yourself in snow that was up to your chest? You would not be able to run, would you? You probably couldn't even walk!

This lucky moose does not have to paw away the snow to get at the plants he likes to eat.

Even in deep snow, elk can often run fast enough to escape the wolves that hunt them.

Musk oxen have heavy, shaggy coats to keep them warm.

If they didn't have dark eyes and noses, this mother polar bear and her cubs would be almost impossible to spot in the snow.

Some animals that don't move away for the winter hibernate instead. Hibernation is a long rest period during which the body's activities slow down. Most bears find a cozy cave or den, curl up, and hibernate until spring. But not polar bears. Except for females who are going to give birth to cubs, they stay active all winter. The females dig dens in the snow and stay in them until after their babies are born in December or January. The mother cares for her babies in the den until they are three months old. As soon as the young polar bear cubs come out of the den, they start playing in the snow. They like to slide down hills. And they very quickly learn from their mother how to scrape away the snow to look for plants they can eat.

Snowshoe hares nibble at branches bent close to the ground by snow.

There are many small creatures who survive the winter by digging burrows right in the snow. Voles, shrews, lemmings, and mice live in these secret places, well hidden from the owls, foxes, and wolves that hunt them. Their burrows and tunnels also protect the food the animals stored in the fall. It may surprise you to know that their snowy rooms also keep them warm. The temperature in their burrows can be as much as 40° Fahrenheit (22° Celsius) warmer than the air temperature above the snow!

Even animals who stay on top of the snow can be helped by it. When heavy snow bends the branches of trees down close to the ground, the snowshoe hare has plenty to eat. It nibbles on the tips of the branches. If the winter snowfalls are so light that the tree branches don't bend down to where the hare can reach them, it might starve to death. It can't dig down through the snow the way larger animals can.

Many small creatures live in burrows that they hollow out of the snow.

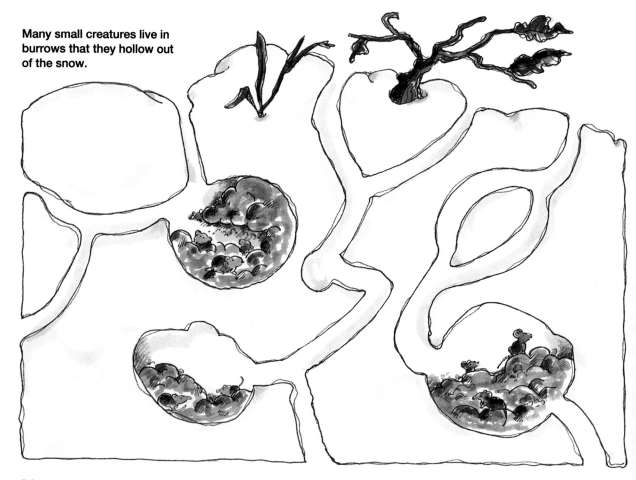

Many animals do just what you do in the wintertime. They put on a heavier coat. Of course, an animal has to grow its own!

There are also animals that wear different-colored coats in the winter from what they wear in the summer. Many kinds of weasels turn white in the winter. So do some rabbits.

A bird that changes color is the ptarmigan (that's pronounced TAR-mi-gan). In warm months ptarmigans are brown and gray. But in the winter they grow a coat of thick white feathers.

Changing color in the winter helps these creatures of the wild escape from their enemies because their white coats make them very hard to see in the snow.

When winter comes, this willow ptarmigan grows a white feather coat.

Snowshoes and Skis

Have you ever tried to walk in deep snow? Unless the snow has a hard frozen crust on the top, you sink way in. You soon get very tired trying to pick your legs up out of snow that is above your knees.

Long ago, people who lived in the far North, where the ground is covered by snow for much of the year, watched animals who could walk on top of the snow. The people figured out that it was the size of the animals' feet that kept them from sinking in. Animals in snow country have big feet which spread their weight out so there is not so much weight in any one spot. Even big animals like musk oxen, which can weigh as much as 900 pounds (400 kilograms), can travel on top of snow crust.

The people decided they could make their own feet bigger by strapping something onto them. They invented snowshoes. They made them from the branches of trees.

You can make yourself a pair of tree-branch snowshoes, too. The best branches to use would be small ones from an evergreen tree because they can easily be bent. Where can you get evergreen branches? Don't just break them off a tree in your yard, or someone else's yard. Even if you are out in the woods, ask an adult about choosing branches so that you don't damage a tree.

Once you learn how, it's easy to walk on top of the snow with snowshoes.

Simple snowshoes can be made out of pieces of wood.

One good place to get evergreen branches is off a live Christmas tree before you dispose of it. The illustrations show how to make snowshoes out of evergreen branches or pieces of lumber.

Be careful when you walk with your snowshoes. Don't let one come down on the edge of the other or you will trip. But at least you will fall in something soft.

It is hard to get up again with snowshoes on your feet, so have someone along to help you.

Using evergreen branches, here's how to make yourself a pair of snowshoes.

With skis strapped to your feet you can travel much faster than you can on snowshoes. Many thousands of years ago, people learned how to glide over the snow on long runners tied to their feet. The very first skis were made from the long bones of animals. They were rubbed and polished so they would slide smoothly.

People soon learned to make skis out of wood. Wooden skis as old as 5,000 years have been found buried in bogs in the far northern lands of Sweden and Norway.

Today skis are made of wood, plastic, fiberglass, or metal.

Walking with skis on snow that covers flat or gently rolling ground is called cross-country skiing.

Unless you are a really good skier don't try going down steep slopes. People who race down mountains on skis sometimes go 100 miles (160 kilometers) an hour!

You're never too young to learn to ski.

"Come on, let's race!"

Experienced downhill skiers can reach speeds as great as 100 miles an hour!

Sleds and Sleighs

If it snows where you live, you have probably swooshed down a snowy hill on a sled. Its metal runners glide smoothly over the snow. Down you rush, to the bottom of the hill. Then you walk back up the hill, pulling your sled.

You don't have to pull a snowmobile up hills. A snowmobile is a sled with an engine to make it move, even up steep slopes.

There are much bigger sleds that are used for hauling heavy loads over snow. In the past such sleds were pulled by horses. Today they are pulled by tractors. In the Arctic, big tractors sometimes pull long trains of sleds.

On their steel runners, sleds move swiftly over the snow.

In a motor-driven snowmobile, you can travel long distances.

During the Christmas season we sing about a time before we had paved roads and automobiles. In those days, people traveled over snow and ice in a kind of sled called a sleigh. It was pulled by a horse with bells on its harness. The bells jingled as the sleigh skimmed over the snow. That is why we sing:

Jingle bells, jingle bells, jingle all the way.

Oh what fun it is to ride in a one-horse open sleigh.

Sleighs were used for more than fun rides in the snow. Winter-time deliveries were often made by sleigh.

In this horse-drawn sleigh, a dairy farmer and his wife are taking a load of milk cans to town where the milk will be sold.

Sled Dogs

In the frozen North, sleds are often pulled by teams of very special dogs. The dogs may be of different breeds but they are all called "sled dogs." They are strong, obedient, and intelligent. They have thick fur to keep them warm, and wide, well-padded feet to help them run on snow. Most carry their tails curled up over their backs so that they don't drag and become crusted with snow.

The explorers who were the first to reach the North and South Poles used sleds pulled by dogs to make their dangerous journeys. In 1909, Robert Peary was the first man to reach the North Pole. Roald Amundsen, in 1911, was the first to reach the South Pole. Neither of these famous expeditions could have been made without sled dogs.

These eager sled dogs are ready to take off on an Arctic adventure.

Today we have other ways to travel in the frozen lands near the earth's poles, but people still train teams of dogs to pull them across snow and ice.

Sled-dog racing is an exciting sport. Every year many drivers and their dog teams take part in a race called the Iditarod Trail Race. The dogs pull their sleds more than a thousand miles through the Alaska wilderness. The race takes many days. When the teams stop to rest, the dogs sleep right out in the snow, with their tails curled up over their noses.

To run the famous Iditarod Trail Race, dogs pull their sleds more than a thousand miles across the Alaskan wilderness.

Can You Keep a Snowflake?

Can you catch a snowflake, take it into your house, and keep it? Well, you can sort of keep it. At least you can keep the shape of it.

Here's how you do it:

You will need a flat piece of glass and a can of the kind of plastic spray artists use on pencil or chalk drawings to keep them from smudging. It is called fixative and you can buy it at any art-supply store.

First keep your piece of glass and can of fixative in the refrigerator for a while so that they are already cold when you take them outside. Carry the glass out in a box or on a piece of cardboard so that it won't get warm from your hand.

Once you are outside, spray the glass with a thin film of fixative. Now catch a snowflake or two on the glass. Quickly hold something above the glass so no more flakes fall on it and pile on top of each other.

To preserve a snowflake, you will need a piece of glass and a can of fixative.

After you catch a snowflake on the pane of glass, cover it quickly.

Go inside with the glass. Don't touch the glass or the snowflakes until the fixative is really dry. That will take about fifteen minutes.

The snowflakes will melt, but their shapes will still be there. They will remain fixed in the plastic for as long as you want to keep them.

You can still see the shape of your snowflake on the Fourth of July!

Index

Alaska, 10, 13, 14, 16, 29
Amundsen, Roald, 28
Animals, change of color
    in winter, 21
Antarctica, 15

Bears
    hibernation, 19
    polar, 15, 19
Blizzards, 11, 31
Burrows in snow, 20

Crystals, 6, 7, 31

Elk, 18
Eskimos, 16, 17

Foxes, 20

Glacier Bay, Alaska, 14
Glaciers, 12–15
Greenland, 15

Hibernation, 19

Ice Age, 12, 31
Iceberg, 31
Iditarod Trail Race, 29
Igloos, 16–17, 31

Lambert-Fisher glacier
    system, 15
Lemmings, 20

Moose, 18
Mt. Rainier, Washington,
    11
Mt. Shasta, California,
    10, 11
    Ski Basin, 11
Musk oxen, 18, 22

North Pole
    expeditions to, 28
    snowfall at, 10

Owls, 20

Peary, Robert, 28
Polar bears, 15, 19
Ptarmigan, 21

Quarayaq glacier, 15

Shrews, 20
Skiing, 24–25
Skis, 24
Sled dogs, 28–29
Sleds, 26
Sled trains, 26
Sleighs, 27, 31
Snow
    Eskimo words for, 17
    measuring depth of, 8–9
    record snowfalls, 11
Snow surveyors, 9
Snowfall
    keeping a record of, 8
    record snowfalls, 11
Snowflakes, 6–7, 34
    preservation of, 30–31
Snowmobile, 26
Snowpack, definition of,
    31
Snowshoe hare, 20
Snowshoes, 22–23
South Pole, 10, 28

Voles, 20

Weasels, 21
Wolves, 18, 20